# BLOODY History of America

## AMERICA'S BLOODY HISTORY
### FROM THE
# CIVIL WAR
### TO THE GREAT
# DEPRESSION

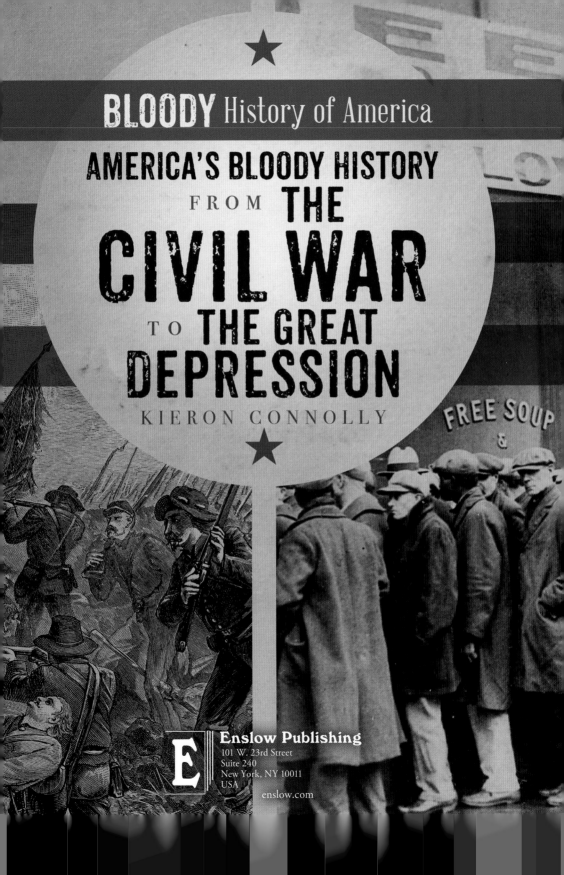

BLOODY History of America

AMERICA'S BLOODY HISTORY
FROM THE
CIVIL WAR
TO THE GREAT
DEPRESSION

KIERON CONNOLLY

**Enslow Publishing**
101 W. 23rd Street
Suite 240
New York, NY 10011
USA

enslow.com

This edition published in 2018 by:

Enslow Publishing, LLC
101 W. 23rd Street, Suite 240
New York, NY 10011

Additional end matter copyright © 2018 by Enslow Publishing, LLC.

© 2018 Amber Books, Ltd.

**Library of Congress Cataloging-in-Publication Data**
Names: Connolly, Kieron, author.
Title: America's bloody history from the Civil War to the Great Depression / Kieron Connolly.
Description: New York, NY : Enslow Publishing, 2018. | Series: Bloody history of America | Includes bibliographical references and index. | Audience: Grades 7–12.
Identifiers: LCCN 2017031475 | ISBN 9780766091788 (library bound) | ISBN 9780766095557 (paperback)
Subjects: LCSH: United States—History—1865–1921—Juvenile literature. | United States—History—Civil War, 1861–1865—Juvenile literature. | United States—History—1919–1933—Juvenile literature.
Classification: LCC E661 .C74 2017 | DDC 973.7—dc23
LC record available at https://lccn.loc.gov/2017031475

Printed in China

**To Our Readers:** We have done our best to make sure all websites in this book were active and appropriate when we went to press. However, the author and the publisher have no control over and assume no liability for the material available on those websites or on any websites they may link to. Any comments or suggestions can be sent by email to customerservice@enslow.com.

**Photo Credits:** Cover (left), pp. 3 (left), 6 ivan-96/DigitalVision Vectors/Getty Images; cover (right), p. 3 (right) Everett Historical/Shutterstock.com; Alamy: 10 (Mary Evans Picture Library), 14 (Painting), 29 (Artokoloro Quint Lox), 31 (Paul Fearn), 35 (Niday Picture Library), 50 (NSF), 58 (World History Archive), 62 (World History Archive), 65 (Pictorial Press), 73 (Heritage Images); Alamy/Granger Collection: 37, 39, 49; Amber Books: 27; Getty Images: 46 (De Agostini), 69 (Moviepix); Getty Images/Archive Photos: 11, 36, 61, 74; Getty Images/Bettmann: 42, 68, 71, 76; Library of Congress: 9, 13, 19–25 all, 40, 41, 45, 51, 54, 57 (Dorothea Lange), 59, 63, 67, 77; U.S. Department of Defense: 17, 30, 52.

# CONTENTS

Introduction ........................................... 7

Chapter 1
The Civil War .......................................... 8

Chapter 2
Freedom and Closing the Frontier ........... 33

Chapter 3
The New Age .......................................... 56

Glossary ................................................. 79

For More Information ............................. 81

Further Reading ..................................... 84

Index ..................................................... 86

A depiction of Pickett's Charge, an infantry assault that Confederate general Robert E. Lee ordered on the last day of the Battle of Gettysburg in July 1863. Brigadier General Lewis Armistead famously led his brigade in the attack with his cap on the end of his sword.

# INTRODUCTION

EVEN THOUGH THE UNITED STATES IS A YOUNG COUNTRY, IT HAS A VASTLY complex history. Conflicts and wars—some very bloody—have played a significant part in shaping the United States as we know it today, and they have marked vastly different chapters in the nation's development.

The story of the United States from the Civil War to the Great Depression is a particularly gruesome one. It involved the institution of slavery, the harsh penalties for those who tried to escape it, and the segregation that followed once it was finally abolished. This period in history also saw the continued ill treatment of Native Americans and the cruelties they suffered during westward expansion.

Domestic issues were especially prevalent during this time as well. Americans grappled with not only racial conflict, changing legislation, and riots, but also with ends and new beginnings, saying goodbye to the Wild West and hello to the rise of Hollywood with its glamour and sordid tales alike. With all of this going on, the United States still eventually joined World War I, losing thousands of lives even though the war was nearly over by the time American soldiers reached the trenches. Moving forward, the early twentieth century saw more industrialization, environmental disasters, and issues such as Prohibition. Then the stock market crashed in 1929, marking the dawn of the Great Depression and causing both people and institutions economic hardship, the likes of which provide valuable lessons for the United States even today.

# CHAPTER 1

# THE CIVIL WAR

GIVEN THE LONG-STANDING DIFFERENCES BETWEEN THE NORTH AND South over slavery, it is less remarkable that they eventually went to war than that violent conflict was avoided for so long. But when war did erupt, the conflict would be particularly bloody, with more American lives lost than in both World Wars combined.

In Georgia in 1848, a slave named Ellen Craft cut her hair short, put on men's clothes and, being light-skinned enough to pass for white, posed as a sickly white gentleman heading north for medical treatment. To complete the picture, accompanying "him" was a black male servant—who was in fact Craft's slave husband, William. In that way, Ellen and William Craft escaped to freedom. Their tale is one of the more remarkable and celebrated regarding fugitive slaves, but throughout the nineteenth century, several hundred slaves a year fled north, assisted by the "underground railroad" of sympathizers.

The Crafts settled in Boston, where William found work as a cabinetmaker. However, two years after their escape, the Fugitive Slave Bill was passed and the Crafts' former slave owner sent two agents to recapture them. With blacks and whites in Boston vehemently opposed to slavery, the Crafts were protected, while the agents were harassed in the streets.

After a couple of days, the pursuers gave up. To some this was "mob law," and President Millard Fillmore denounced the actions of the Bostonians. Meanwhile, the Crafts' friends helped them onto a ship bound for England.

The Crafts had escaped again, but in the 1850s, there were 332 cases of alleged former slaves being forcibly returned to the South. Some had fled north years earlier, but in February 1851, a black man was taken from his wife and family in southern Indiana and returned to an owner who claimed that he was a slave who had run away nearly 20 years before. The burden of proof lay with the man to prove that he was free, not with the agents to prove he was the slave they were seeking. In response to the new law, many people in northern black communities fled across the border to Canada—an estimated 3,000 moving there in 1850 alone.

BATTLE OF WILLIAMSBURG.

During the Civil War, the North had a larger population, more industry, control of the US Navy, and more than three times the number of white men of military age. The South, though, had some international support, notably from Britain.

## VIOLENT PROTESTS

"Civil War—The First Blow Struck" read a headline in a Lancaster, Pennsylvania, newspaper in September 1851—more than a decade before the Civil War broke out. The story reported how a slave owner had ventured north to recapture two slaves and had been shot dead on encountering armed resistance from 24 free blacks. To the South, this was an act of insurrection supported by fanatics, and President Fillmore sent in the Marines. Although several arrests were made of both black and white men, charges were later dropped.

Fugitive slave Ellen Craft disguised herself as a sickly white man as part of the escape she and her husband made when they fled to Boston in 1848. When agents were sent to recapture them, the Crafts were protected by free blacks and white sympathizers.

Not that the North was universally in favor of abolition. Former slaves moving into free communities in northern cities were repeatedly attacked by mobs, as in Providence, Rhode Island, in 1831; a decade later the black population was expelled from Cincinnati.

While defenders of slavery in the South argued that, unlike wage earners who might risk unemployment and even starvation, slaves were looked after for life, the abolitionist movement in the North among whites and blacks continued to grow.

Not that everything was straightforward among some abolitionists. While slavery might well be considered a moral abomination, self-interest could complicate anti-slavery feeling. Some people worried: would the spread of slavery result in more slaves fleeing to free states, and, thus, in competing for jobs, push down wages? Would slave states develop more competitive manufacturing industries than Northern states? Or would slave plantations become established in the West to rival free farms? The debate raged back and forth across the states.

# $500, REWARD.

**Ran away from the undersigned, on Sunday the 9th inst., a negro boy named**

## AARON or APE.

He is about **20** years old, six feet high, with rather unusually large legs and arms; walks bent forward with one foot turned out more than the other. I will give **$150,00** reward for him if taken in the county; **$100,00** reward if taken in the counties south of this and **$200,00** if taken in any of the Mississippi counties or **$500** if taken out of the State.

### O. M. HARRIS,

**Three miles south of Midddle Grove Monroe Coounty, Missouri.**

REGISTER PRINT—MACON CITY, MO.

A $500 reward offered for a runaway slave from Missouri named "Aaron or Ape." In the 1850s, there were 332 cases of alleged former slaves being forcibly returned from free states to the South under the Fugitive Slave Law.

## BLEEDING KANSAS

The Missouri Compromise of 1820 had stated that all states north of the 36 degrees 30 line were barred from slavery, but by the 1850s this was being undermined. The Compromise of 1850 allowed Utah Territory, all of which was north of the line, to choose whether or not it should be a "free" state. Meanwhile, California, most of which lay *south* of the line, had chosen to enter the Union as such.

Then, in 1853, Democratic Senator Stephen A. Douglas's Kansas-Nebraska Act allowed the new territories of Kansas and Nebraska—both of which were north of the line and had been carved out of what had previously been termed "permanent" Native American territory—to settle their slavery issue by popular vote. Many in the North feared that slavery would now expand across the West.

In response to the act, a new political player, the Republican Party, emerged. While Whigs and Democrats had support across the North and South, Republicans were dedicated to stopping slavery's further expansion. In time, the party would be joined by Abraham Lincoln, a former Whig congressman and lawyer working in Illinois.

With both pro-slavery and anti-slavery factions moving into Kansas to swing the state their way, violent conflict erupted there, with pro-slavery forces burning the free-soil town of Lawrence in 1856. In response, Massachusetts abolitionist John Brown led a group that killed five pro-slavery settlers near Pottawatomie Creek, in Franklin County. Armed anti-abolitionists took over polling stations, casting fraudulent ballots to elect a pro-slavery legislature, and guerrilla fighting spread quickly across the state, resulting in 200 deaths.

**ARMED ANTI-ABOLITIONISTS TOOK OVER POLLING STATIONS, CASTING FRAUDULENT BALLOTS.**

The question was, could, or would, the Supreme Court reinforce the Missouri Compromise? Alas, no. In 1857, the case of Dred Scott came up. As a slave who had been taken to the

Dred Scott's case arguing for his freedom from slavery caused public outrage and deepened tensions between the North and South when it was rejected by the Supreme Court in 1857.

free territory of Minnesota, was he free and therefore exempt from later sale as a chattel? The Supreme Court decided that not only was Scott not free, but that Congress had no right to forbid slavery in the territories, and that, as a non-citizen, Scott had no right to sue. With that decision, slavery was free to expand. The Missouri Compromise had been repealed.

John Brown was found guilty of murder, treason against the Commonwealth of Virginia, and inciting a slave rebellion. Although fitting his character, it is a myth that he kissed a black child on his way to the gallows.

## JOHN BROWN'S BODY

Fanatic? Murderer? Prophet? John Brown's violent protests against slavery were condemned by some in both the North and the South. His final action was an attempt to establish liberated zones in the hills of western Virginia, by leading 18 followers, five of whom were black, against a federal arsenal at Harper's Ferry in October 1859. Hoping to spark a slave revolt, his raid was

**JOHN BROWN'S RAID WAS A MESS AND MOST OF HIS MEN WERE SOON KILLED OR CAPTURED.**

a mess; within two days, most of his men had been killed or captured. He received the death penalty, a punishment that inevitably made him a martyr for the abolitionist cause.

Tensions rose across the country in 1860, with mob attacks on suspected abolitionists, and boycotts against northern goods, while in Texas a vigilante outbreak resulted in the deaths of a hundred suspected dissidents. In November of that year, Republican candidate Abraham Lincoln won the presidential election—unsurprisingly gaining virtually no seats in the South. With an anti-slavery party now in power, South Carolina seceded from the Union, followed by the Deep South states of Mississippi, Alabama, Louisiana, Georgia, Florida, and Texas. In February 1861, the Confederate States of America were born.

## PRESIDENT LINCOLN

Lincoln's presidency not only ended in an assassination, it began with his efforts to avoid one. Fearing an attack by pro-slavery vigilantes before his inauguration, he disguised himself as an invalid to travel on a special train through Philadelphia and Baltimore, arriving before dawn in the capital for the ceremony. It was an inauspicious beginning to a presidency that would see the Union torn apart and then recast as free to all black people.

Not that Lincoln was a dogmatic abolitionist. His two basic aims in the war were to stop the further expansion of slavery westwards and to preserve the Union. "I have no purpose, directly or indirectly, to interfere with the institution of slavery in the States where it exists," he said in his inaugural address in March 1861. "We are not enemies," he said of the Confederacy, "but friends…," even though the new Confederacy had already elected Jefferson Davis as its president.

## GOING TO WAR

Statistically, the North had a huge advantage over the South. It had twice the population, vastly more industry, more railways, 75 percent of the nation's farmland, 16,000 men in its army, and 90 warships. In sum, it controlled 75 percent of the country's wealth.

The only hope for the first seven Confederate states was in enlisting the help of the Upper South—the more northerly, industrialized states— in particular Virginia. That way, it might be able to drag out the conflict long enough for the North to become war-weary and give in to secession.

However, even in a conflict about slavery, the issues were not always clear-cut: Kentucky, Maryland, and Missouri were border states in the Union that were also slave-owning. Meanwhile, in areas of the South with few or no slaves, such as the Appalachian uplands, there was Unionist sentiment.

## FIRST BLOOD

The opening shots of the war were an artillery bombardment from Charleston, South Carolina, at Fort Sumter—a federal property commanded by Major Robert Anderson. With few supplies, Anderson could hold out for only a day and a half before he had to surrender.

The fall of Fort Sumter was sufficient to persuade Virginia to secede. Arkansas, North Carolina, and Tennessee followed, making a total of 11 Confederate states. Who, though, was to lead them?

Lincoln had offered command of the Union army to Robert E. Lee, but Lee found his loyalties divided: although devoted to the Union, he was a

Confederate soldiers occupy Fort Sumter, Charleston, South Carolina, after the surrender of the Union Army in the war's first engagement. Crucially for the Confederates, this victory persuaded the more industrialized state of Virginia to side with them.

Virginian. After much anguish, he resigned his commission in the Union Army and rode south to Richmond, Virginia, the new Confederate capital, and little more than 100 miles (160 kilometers) from Washington. There he accepted the command of the Confederate Army.

## BULL RUN

The first true battle of the Civil War came in July 1861 at Bull Run Creek, just 25 miles (40 km) from Washington. With ill-prepared Union soldiers, many of whom were nearing the end of the 90-day term for which they had signed up, the battle quickly turned into a rout when the Confederates surged forward. Many Union troops drowned trying to cross Bull Run Creek: it was a humiliating defeat for the Union. But Bull

## SLAVES IN THE CAPITAL

In the 1840s, the District of Columbia (D.C.)—which encompasses Washington—still had a thriving slave market in its city of Alexandria. Fearing abolition, D.C.'s pro-slavery residents petitioned Virginia to take back the land, including Alexandria, that it had donated to help form the District in the 1790s. With Congress in agreement, in July 1846 that land was returned to Virginia. The Compromise of 1850 abolished the slave trade in D.C., though not slavery itself. That lasted until the Civil War, when, in 1862, slaves there were emancipated, with slaveholders receiving up to $300 per freed slave. Each newly freed slave was given $100 if he or she chose to settle in places such as Haiti or Liberia—the idea persisting that the US was a white society and blacks might be better off abroad. Some blacks were also compensated as slave owners, having once bought their family members away from other owners. In all, 3,185 slaves in D.C. were freed.

Run (or Manassas, as it is also known) did prompt the North to take the war more seriously.

## GRANT AND SHILOH

Robert E. Lee had been lost to the Union when war broke out. Ulysses S. Grant, who would become the other great leader of the war, wasn't even in the Union Army, let alone leading a unit. Grant was a former soldier who had been thrown out of the army for drinking; failing to find any other purpose in life, he was selling leather goods in his father's shop in Illinois. Now the army needed him back.

By 1862, Grant was a brigadier general, making his name at the Battle of Shiloh in Tennessee—although it didn't begin well for him. On the first morning of the battle, April 6, the Confederates surprised the

Unionists, who, though fighting on, were driven back in disarray. It was a disaster for the North. However, thousands of reinforcements arrived overnight, and the following morning it was the Unionists' turn to push the exhausted Confederates off the battlefield. The death toll was immense: about 13,000 Union troops were killed, while the Confederates lost about 10,500. In fact, more Americans died at Shiloh than in all the country's previous wars combined.

Despite the Union victory at Shiloh, by the summer things were looking so promising for the South that Lee invaded the North, hoping that it might

**MORE AMERICANS DIED AT SHILOH THAN IN ALL THE COUNTRY'S PREVIOUS WARS COMBINED.**

result in Britain recognizing the Confederacy. If, as Lincoln said, the war was about preserving the Union, not about freeing slaves, then secession

The Battle of Shiloh, in Tennessee in April 1862, began as a disaster for the Unionists when they were surprised by Confederate forces. But, having been reinforced overnight, the Unionists pushed the exhausted Confederates off the battlefield the following day.

could be regarded internationally as a fight for independence from an overbearing empire. Furthermore, Britain depended on plantation cotton to supply its textile industry and was already sufficiently sympathetic to the Confederate cause to allow it to build warships in British dockyards.

Lee's advance into Maryland, however, found the Unionists better prepared than expected. At the Battle of Antietam (Sharpsburg) on September 17, the Union soldiers were victorious. However, losses were again huge on both sides—the combined casualties of killed and wounded reaching 23,000, making it the bloodiest single-day battle in American history. Lee's army was

## ANTIETAM REMAINS THE BLOODIEST SINGLE-DAY BATTLE IN AMERICAN HISTORY.

now too weak to continue its campaign. Emboldened, Lincoln elevated the conflict into something more than just preserving the Union.

## THE EMANCIPATION PROCLAMATION

Before Antietam, there had been a chance that border states might switch to the Confederacy, but now the Unionists were on a stronger footing. Five days after the battle, Lincoln issued a preliminary emancipation proclamation, promising to free blacks in rebel-held areas from January 1, 1863. Internationally, this proved the death knell for any possible support for the Confederacy: while Britain might have backed the South in the name of freedom fighters, it definitely would not send troops to defend slavery.

Confederate President Jefferson Davis called the proclamation "a measure by which several millions of human beings of an inferior race, peaceful and contented laborers in their sphere, are doomed to extermination, while at the same time they are encouraged to a general assassination of their masters." That was, perhaps, an expected response. However, Lincoln had other worries when, in a backlash in the North, hundreds of soldiers deserted, and, in the 1862 elections, those Democrats pushing for a peace settlement with the Confederates leaped to 32 seats in the House.

# ABRAHAM LINCOLN
## AND HIS
# Emancipation Proclamation

**Whereas** On the Twenty-second day of September, in the year of our Lord one thousand eight hundred and sixty-two, a Proclamation was issued by the President of the United States, containing among other things the following, to-wit:

"That on the first day of January, in the year of our Lord one thousand eight hundred and sixty-three, all persons held as slaves within any State, or designated part of a State, the people whereof shall then be in rebellion against the United States, shall be then, thenceforward and forever free, and the executive government of the United States, including the military and naval authority thereof, will recognize and maintain the freedom of such persons, and will do no act or acts to repress such persons, or any of them, in any efforts they may make for their actual freedom.

"That the executive will, on the first day of January aforesaid, by proclamation, designate the States and parts of States, if any, in which the people thereof respectively shall then be in rebellion against the United States, and the fact that any State, or the people thereof, shall on that day be in good faith represented in the Congress of the United States by members chosen thereto at elections wherein a majority of the qualified voters of such State shall have participated, shall, in the absence of strong countervailing testimony, be deemed conclusive evidence that such State and the people thereof are not then in rebellion against the United States."

Now, therefore, I, ABRAHAM LINCOLN, President of the United States, by virtue of the power in me vested as Commander-in-Chief of the Army and Navy of the United States in time of actual armed rebellion against the authority and government of the United States, and as a fit and necessary war measure for suppressing said rebellion, do, on this first day of January, in the year of our Lord one thousand eight hundred and sixty-three, and in accordance with my purpose so to do, publicly proclaim for the full period of one hundred days from the day the first above mentioned order, and designate as the States and parts of States wherein the people thereof respectively are this day in rebellion against the United States, the following, to-wit:

ARKANSAS, TEXAS, LOUISIANA (except the parishes of St. Bernard, Plaquemines, Jefferson, St. John, St. Charles, St. James, Ascension, Assumption, Terre Bonne, Lafourche, St. Mary, St. Martin, and Orleans, including the city of New Orleans), MISSISSIPPI, ALABAMA, FLORIDA, GEORGIA, SOUTH CAROLINA, NORTH CAROLINA and VIRGINIA (except the forty-eight counties designated as West Virginia, and also the counties of Berkley, Accomac, Northampton, Elizabeth City, York, Princess Ann and Norfolk, including the cities of Norfolk and Portsmouth), and which excepted parts are, for the present, left precisely as if this Proclamation were not issued.

And by virtue of the power and for the purpose aforesaid, I do order and declare that all persons held as slaves within said designated States and parts of States are and henceforward shall be free; and that the executive government of the United States, including the military and naval authorities thereof, will recognize and maintain the freedom of said persons.

And I hereby enjoin upon the people so declared to be free, to abstain from all violence, unless in necessary self-defence, and I recommend to them that in all cases, when allowed, they labor faithfully for reasonable wages.

And I further declare and make known that such persons of suitable condition, will be received into the armed service of the United States to garrison forts, positions, stations and other places, and to man vessels of all sorts in said service.

And upon this act, sincerely believed to be an act of justice, warranted by the Constitution, upon military necessity, I invoke the considerate judgment of mankind, and the gracious favor of Almighty God.

In testimony whereof, I have hereunto set my name, and caused the seal of the United States to be affixed.

Done at the City of Washington, this first day of January, in the year of our Lord one thousand eight hundred and sixty-three, and of the Independence of the United States the eighty-Seventh.

By the President:                                        ABRAHAM LINCOLN.

WILLIAM H. SEWARD, Secretary of State.

NOTE.—The rest of the slaves were afterwards freed by Legislation and Constitutional Amendments.

Overall, though, across the South, the slave system was already beginning to crumble; with white masters away fighting, many slaves fled north or went on go-slows. To maintain order, when conscription was introduced in the South, those owning more than 20 slaves were exempt.

## BLACK SOLDIERS IN THE UNION ARMY

In January 1863, Lincoln went a step further, declaring that freed slaves would be received into the Union's armed forces. While his motivations were partly to solve a manpower shortage, the move had wider ramifications. "Once let the black man get upon his person the brass letter," said former slave and campaigner Frederick Douglass, "there is no power on earth that can deny that he has earned the right to citizenship."

Free blacks and former slaves rushed to join up, amounting to nearly a tenth of the Union Army by the end of the war. Unsurprisingly, inequalities remained, and, until they complained, black soldiers earned $3 less a month than white ones, while, still suffering discrimination, they mostly fought in segregated units and in the lower ranks. Furthermore, if they were captured by the Confederates, they could be tried as slave insurrectionists—an offense that carried the death penalty.

## THE BATTLE OF GETTYSBURG

Following a devastating defeat of Union forces at Fredericksburg in Virginia in December 1862, General Lee had a successful spring in 1863. He ran rings around the Union Army, before venturing into the North and invading Pennsylvania. What black civilians the Confederates found there were sent south into slavery.

At this point, however, Lee's army ran into General George Meade's Union forces near a small town called Gettysburg. Preparing for battle, Meade settled the Union line along low ridges. It was a strong position, but Lee, brimming with confidence after his recent victories, was not deterred. After two days of episodic fighting, on July 3, Lee ordered his men to march forward towards the Union line, even though that meant moving across a mile of open farmland against an enemy dug in on higher ground and backed by artillery. As the Confederates advanced, the Union soldiers waited with their weapons loaded until the enemy was a couple of hundred yards away. They then fired 1700 rifles at the same time, backed by 11 cannons.

In 1863, African Americans were accepted into the Union forces. By the end of the war, more than 200,000 were serving in the Union Army and Navy.

Barely any Confederate soldiers reached the Union lines—and only half of the 15,000 advancing men made it back to their own lines. Not only was the battle lost for the Confederates, after that day Lee's forces were unable to pursue the campaign. They turned back to Virginia.

## THE GETTYSBURG ADDRESS

It took months to clear away the bodies at Gettysburg, but that November a special cemetery for Union dead was opened. Edward Everett, a celebrated orator, gave a two-hour speech, which Lincoln was requested to follow with "a few appropriate remarks." In all, he spoke 272 words, including these: "the world will little note nor long remember what we say here." He was wrong about that. In the Gettysburg Address, as his speech became known, Lincoln, from the opening, "Four score and seven years ago," to the

**IN JUST 272 WORDS IN THE GETTYSBURG ADDRESS, LINCOLN REDEFINED THE WAR.**

closing, "government of the people, by the people, for the people...," redefined the war. He didn't mention the Union or Confederacy once, but said "nation" five times—a word not used in the Declaration of Independence, which had referred to "Free and Independent States." Also, he anchored the speech in the values of the American Revolution—a fight for equality and liberty—while not talking about slavery specifically. As historian James M. McPherson has noted, it was after the Gettysburg Address that people largely shifted from saying, "The United States are," to "The United States is...."

Given at the opening of a cemetery for Union dead in November 1863, Lincoln's Gettysburg Address reaffirmed the republic's foundations in liberty, proclaiming that "a new birth of freedom" would bring equality to all the nation's citizens.

# SUBMARINES AND BALLOONS

The Civil War witnessed a number of technological advances that would change warfare. The immense number of casualties at Antietam in 1862, for instance, was due to new rifles that were far more accurate, and their range four times greater, than earlier muskets.

The conflict also prefigured World War I with drawn-out battles fought from trenches, such as at Vicksburg, Mississippi (May–July 1863), where the Confederates were starved into submission, and at Petersburg, Virginia (June 1864–March 1865).

In naval warfare, the conflict saw the first ironclads—steam-powered, iron-hulled ships. USS *Monitor* is best known for its central role in the Battle of Hampton Roads, Virginia, in March 1862, where it was the first ironclad to encounter and defeat another ironclad—CSS *Virginia*. With a revolving turret, *Monitor*'s design would establish a type of warship in its name.

Although they might seem to be an invention of the twentieth century, early submarines played a small role in the conflict, too. CSS *Hunley* was a 40 ft. (12 m) submarine, powered by a crew of seven hand-cranking the propeller. Reaching a speed of 4.6 mph (7.4 km/h) and armed with one torpedo, in February 1864 the *Hunley* attacked and sank the warship USS *Housatonic*, which had been part of the Union blockade of Charleston. On its way back to base, however, the *Hunley* sank, with all lives lost.

Existing technologies were also put to military use. Hot-air balloons would ascend over a battlefield; then, with wires hooked up to telegraph lines, positions could be telegraphed back to commanders.

There were non-military developments, too. The Union imposed the country's first income tax and issued the first paper currency, enabling it to endure the conflict with less inflation than the South. The war also led to the revoking of some US liberties: arrest without trial was allowed, while martial law was imposed in war areas in both the North and South.

An observation balloon at Seven Pines, Virginia, in May 1862. With the balloon connected to telegraph wires, enemy positions could be telegrammed back to commanders.

## BATTLE OF FORT PILLOW

In April 1864, Confederate General Bedford Forrest led his forces in attacking Fort Pillow, Tennessee, where the Union garrison consisted of 585 men, half of them black. While some on both sides claimed that the Union Army never gave in and fought to the end, the majority view from Unionists and Confederates was that the battle turned into a massacre after the Union Army had surrendered.

The Confederates suffered only 14 fatalities, but the Union lost 277 men, 80 percent of whom were black. Were more blacks killed in the fighting simply because of where they were positioned at the fort? Or was it a case that, fearing enslavement if they surrendered, they fought to the death? Or were they specifically targeted by the Confederates? Some certainly did surrender: one Confederate soldier, writing home soon after the battle, described how "deluded negroes would run up to our men, fall upon their knees, and with uplifted hand scream for mercy, but were ordered to their feet and then shot down." Would they have shot dead a white Union soldier who had surrendered?

Lincoln discussed the massacre with his Cabinet, wondering if he should enforce an Order of Retaliation, by which any Confederate prisoner of war would be executed if a Union prisoner were killed, and put on hard labor any POW if a Union soldier were enslaved.

In the end, no action was taken, although the Joint Committee on the Conduct of the War investigated the events. In the South, General Forrest regarded the losses at Fort Pillow as demonstrating "to the Northern people that negro soldiers cannot cope with Southerners." He later became the Grand Wizard of the Ku Klux Klan.

## NEW YORK RIOTS

John D. Rockefeller, J.P. Morgan, and Andrew Carnegie all began making their names during the Civil War—but in business, not on the battlefield. With conscription introduced in the North in the spring of 1863,

THE FORT PILLOW MASSACRE.

At Fort Pillow, 80 percent of the Union dead were black, although they represented only half of the Union forces present.

each legitimately paid at least $300 to be exempted from military service. For $850, Carnegie paid an Irish immigrant to take his place.

The inequality of the conscription laws did not go unnoticed, and, just weeks after the victory at Gettysburg, riots erupted in New York. In what was perhaps also an expression of war-weariness, more than 100 people were killed when largely Irish crowds attacked the black population, abolitionists, and draft offices. Other attacks rippled across the North.

## APPROACHING ATLANTA

Gettysburg may in hindsight be seen as a turning point in the war, but victory was by no means certain for the North. Ulysses S. Grant was now in charge of the Union armies and was seeking a victory in Virginia, but at Cold Harbor in June 1864, thousands were lost in an advance on Confederate trenches, with 6,000 killed in a single hour. In the same month, the Union suffered 50,000 dead or wounded in other battles, and the outskirts of Washington were attacked. At Petersburg, Grant's campaign turned into nine months of trench warfare with lines extending more than 30 miles (48 km) to the outskirts of Richmond.

By the summer of 1864, it was unsurprising that Lincoln did not think he would be re-elected in November. As it happened, General William Tecumseh

**AT PETERSBURG, GRANT'S CAMPAIGN TURNED INTO NINE MONTHS OF TRENCH WARFARE.**

Sherman's force came to the rescue. Approaching from Tennessee, Sherman besieged Atlanta, before setting it on fire. He then continued a scorched earth policy until he reached the coast. The morale boost of Sherman's success helped Lincoln be re-elected.

## CONFEDERATE SLAVE SOLDIERS

By 1864, the South was crumbling internally. The Northern blockade on European imports was having its effect, printing money was leading to roaring inflation, and starving soldiers were beginning to desert. The result was that by early 1865, the Confederates had begun to think the unthinkable: could they put slaves in the army in return for offering them their freedom? For four years they had fought to preserve slavery and now it was being suggested that they free the slaves. Southerners were bitterly divided on the matter, but General Lee was in favor of having them serve. "We must decide whether slavery shall be extinguished by our enemies and the slaves be used against us," he said, "or use them ourselves at the risk of the effects." Of course, by making black men soldiers, as Frederick Douglass had argued in the North, you made them citizens. As General Howell Cobb from Georgia pointed out: "If slaves will make good soldiers, our whole theory of slavery is wrong." Desperation won the argument: blacks were accepted into the Confederate Army in March.

Two months earlier, Lincoln had succeeded in pushing the Thirteenth Amendment through Congress, ending slavery by just two votes. Many had defended slavery as part of their constitutional rights, but now the Constitution had been changed and those who might object—the Southerners—were not part of Congress to protest.

Protesting at the unfairness of the conscription laws—where the wealthy could pay to be exempt—riots erupted in New York in July 1863. Draft offices, blacks, and abolitionists were attacked, with at least 100 lives lost.

The hanging at Arsenal Prison, Washington, DC, on July 7, 1865, of four of John Wilkes Booth's fellow conspirators in the assassination of President Lincoln.

## APPOMATTOX

By April, the Confederates could no longer defend their capital, Richmond. Fires were lit as government papers were burned and supply depots were ignited. Confederate forces abandoned the city; on April 4, Lincoln entered the smoldering ruins to a cheering crowd of black people. After a short battle in the village of Appomattox Court House five days later, General Robert E. Lee surrendered.

On April 14, Lincoln and his wife Mary took their seats in the presidential box at Ford's Theatre in Washington to see a comedy. During the play, the president was shot in the back of the head at point-blank range by John Wilkes Booth. The assassin then jumped down to the stage, shouting, "*Sic semper tyrannis!*" ("So is it always for tyrants")—the motto of Virginia—before fleeing. Booth, an actor who was part of a plot to save the Confederacy, was tracked down 12 days later and, refusing to surrender, shot dead.

A national day of mourning marked Lincoln's funeral. After that, his coffin began the long, meandering journey back to his hometown of Springfield, Illinois, with funeral services in different cities along the way. It is estimated that half a million people in Philadelphia went to pay their respects.

## IN INDIAN COUNTRY

As with the War of Independence, Native Americans fought—almost 29,000 of them—on both sides in the Civil War. Once again, they suffered greatly, with more than 10,000 killed. Despite the South having removed them to the West, generally the "Five Civilized Tribes" retained strong ties with Southern states, directing their hostility towards the Union. The Cherokee, however, were divided and ended up fighting their own civil war. The primary dispute was between Chief John Ross and Stand Watie, both of whom were slave owners who represented different Cherokee populations: Ross's followers were poorer; Watie's were wealthier farmers. Watie became a brigadier-general in the Confederacy, while Ross's men, led by his nephew John Drew, defected north to Unionist Kansas in 1862. The following year Ross joined them and freed his own slaves.

Watie's forces fought many winning battles against Unionist Creek and Cherokee. But after the war, the Cherokee farmlands were in ruins and, devoid of a governing structure, remained violent and anarchic.

## HOME OF THE BRAVE

In all, somewhere between 620,000 and 750,000 lives were lost in the Civil War, while hundreds of thousands of men were maimed. Although large parts of the Southern states were untouched by the fighting, Atlanta and Richmond were in ruins, as were many farms. The South had seceded from the Union over slavery, and rejoining it would mean accepting the Thirteenth Amendment.

Lincoln had been a moderate abolitionist, and not, originally, in favor of an equal standing between the races. In 1858, he had declared

**BETWEEN 620,000 AND 750,000 LIVES WERE LOST IN THE CIVIL WAR.**

himself opposed to: "the social and political equality of the white and black races," "making voters or jurors of negroes," and to black people "intermarry[ing] with white people."

Now he had succeeded in making slaves free. But, killed at the pinnacle of his achievements, he would escape the burden of bringing the Union together again and making emancipation work.

# CHAPTER 2

# FREEDOM AND CLOSING THE FRONTIER

IN THE SOUTH, SLAVES WERE NOW FREE, BUT LIBERTY WOULD throw up new barriers. Meanwhile, in the North, corruption and the exploitation of the workers helped industry to boom, and, in the West, the days of being wild were nearing their end.

A third of the South had been badly affected by the Civil War, but the rest was largely untouched. The great challenge now lay in reconciling the South with the North politically, and in creating a new economy no longer based on slave labor. As it was impossible to try every Confederate as a traitor, it was agreed that a state could be readmitted to the Union once a certain proportion of its citizens had taken an oath of loyalty to the United States. By the end of 1865, state governments founded on these principles were in place in the South.

Freed slaves were happy to walk away from their plantations, but now four million free men and women—conditioned all their lives to slavery—had to find their way in the world with no property, no education and little or no money. A former slave was, said former abolitionist Frederick Douglass, "free from the individual master but the slave of society."

Although the Thirteenth Amendment had liberated slaves, within months most Southern states had passed legal codes aimed at keeping black people in subordination. They were denied the right to vote or to serve on juries, and they could not testify against white people either. The Second Amendment was also refused to them—that is, they were not given the right to bear arms.

To counteract the behavior of the states, Congress passed the Civil Rights Act, giving full citizenship to blacks, which became permanent in the Fourteenth Amendment in June 1866. Ten years earlier, the Supreme Court had declared that Dred Scott and all other blacks were not citizens. Now, according to American law, "all persons born or naturalized in the United States were citizens."

Still dominated by Northern states, Congress passed legislation to dissolve Southern state governments in 1867 and put the South under peacetime military rule until it was decided that they were cooperating. With such backing, all state legislatures in the South had, for the first time, black members. In the most extreme example, of the 123 members of South Carolina's House of Representatives in 1873, 100

**MORE THAN 3,000 PEOPLE, MAINLY BLACK, WERE KILLED OR WOUNDED IN BATTLES AND MASSACRES IN LOUISIANA.**

were black. In elections, blacks had the vote, while whites who had supported the Confederacy did not. For a time, black votes outnumbered white ones. And free public education was introduced for all across the South.

An 1868 campaign poster portraying the Democratic Party as opposed to the Reconstruction and black rights while favoring the interests of: Irish Americans (*left*), Southern Confederates as represented by Nathan Bedford Forrest (*center*), and northern businessmen, represented by financier August Belmont (*right*).

## KU KLUX KLAN

The reconstruction of the South became a great opportunity for political reform—but also, for some, for profiteering. Carpetbaggers—northerners who lived out of a suitcase and were only in town long enough to rip off someone, and scalawags—southern fellow travellers—together managed to exploit the public offices of the South through corruption and bribery.

Soon opposition to Republican rule, especially where crooks and conmen had moved in, led to the rise in Tennessee in 1866 of the Ku Klux Klan. With its members dressed in white robes and hoods, the Klan sought to terrorize black and white supporters of the Republican

A Prospective Scene in the "City of Oaks," 4th of March, 1869.

" Hang, curs, hang! * * * * *  *Their* complexion is perfect gallows.  Stand fast, good fate, to *their* hanging! * * * * * If they be not born to be hanged, our case is miserable."

The above cut represents the fate in store for those great pests of Southern society—the carpet-bagger and scallawag—if found in Dixie's Land after the break of day on the 4th of March next.

An 1868 political cartoon published in Alabama's *Tuscaloosa Independent Monitor*, which was edited by local Ku Klux Klan leader Ryland Randolph. The cartoon threatens that carpetbaggers and scalawags seeking to profit from the South will be hanged.

Party and thereby help get a Democrat into the White House. The Klan was outlawed within five years, but in that time it had stretched its purpose to include that of police force, judge, jury, and executioner. When former slave Cy Guy was believed to have made a "scandalous insult" to a white woman in Orange County, North Carolina, the Klan came after him. "They tries him there in the woods," remembered former slave Ben Johnson. Then they strung him up, writing in Guy's own blood, "that any nigger what takes down the body shall be hunged too." Only after four days did the sheriff remove the body.

There were similar white revolutionary movements in other parts of the South. In 1874, several thousand supporters of the White League attempted an armed revolt in New Orleans. In total, in the decade to 1876, more than 3,000 people, mainly black, were killed or wounded in battles and massacres in Louisiana.

One by one, the Republican state governments of the South began to fall, being replaced by regimes reflecting traditional Southern power: white landowners. By 1877, the Reconstruction that had begun at the

A camp of freed slaves in the former Confederate capital of Richmond, Virginia, in 1865.

end of the Civil War was ending. Then in 1883, the Supreme Court over-turned the Civil Rights Act of 1875, which had guaranteed black access to public places. Blacks also lost their voting rights through devices such as literacy tests and poll taxes, meaning that between 1896 and 1904 the number of registered black voters in Louisiana fell from 130,000 to just 1,350. Those imprisoned might find themselves laboring as convicts or on the chain gang—"corporate public slavery in all but name," as historian Philip Jenkins describes it.

## SHARECROPPING AND SEGREGATION

Most blacks and many whites could not afford to farm their own land, so they received plots from landowners, who gave them half of their crop in a system known as sharecropping. As the former slaves lacked the cash to get started, landowners loaned them seed and equipment on credit, driving them into debt. Furthermore, being illiterate, many former slaves were open to exploitation by the sharp practice of some landowners regarding the contracts they were asked to agree to. Some virtually re-enslaved themselves through documents they unwittingly signed. "For many black laborers and sharecroppers," writes historian David Reynolds, "the New South was little better than the Old."

Where the old division had been between slave and free, in the New South the division came between black and white. "Jim Crow" laws, as they became known, separated black and white people in public places. On trains, the Jim Crow car was the hot, dirty one next to the engine. When, in 1895, Homer Plessy deliberately sat in a whites-only part of a Louisiana train, he was arrested and jailed.

Plessy managed to take his case to the Supreme Court, arguing equal rights for all citizens under the Fourteenth Amendment. However, his case was rejected, with the Court stating that the Amendment "could not have been intended to abolish distinctions based upon color, or to enforce social, as distinguished from political, equality." In the same ruling, the

Court affirmed that segregation was legal as long as separate facilities were equal in quality, leaving it to individual states to ensure that standards of equality were maintained. They were not. Slavery had been replaced by segregation.

## BIG CITY CORRUPTION

The final third of the nineteenth century was, in the words of historian Philip Jenkins, a "time of buccaneering capitalism at its most flagrant." Andrew Carnegie and John D. Rockefeller may now be remembered as great philanthropists, but they were ruthless when it came to forging their way ahead in the American steel and oil industries. Similarly, the "Erie Ring" of financiers Daniel Drew, Jim Fisk, and Jay Gould—flush from their successes profiteering and blockade running during the Civil War—challenged Cornelius Vanderbilt over his efforts to monopolize the transportation systems of New York State. Both sides played dirty, fighting their battle with thugs, as well as through immense bribery of the courts, judges, and public officials.

Politics had become corrupt, too. Between 1866 and 1871, New York City

# JIM CROW LAW.

## UPHELD BY THE UNITED STATES SUPREME COURT.

### Statute Within the Competency of the Louisiana Legislature and Railroads—Must Furnish Separate Cars for Whites and Blacks.

Washington, May 18.—The Supreme Court today in an opinion read by Justice Brown, sustained the constitutionality of the law in Louisiana requiring the railroads of that State to provide separate cars for white and colored passengers. There was no interstate, commerce feature in the case for the railroad upon which the incident occurred giving rise to case—Plessey vs. Ferguson—East Louisiana railroad, was and is operated wholly within the State, to the laws of Congress of many of the States. The opinion states that by the analogy of the laws of Congress, and of many of states requiring establishment of separate schools for children of two races and other similar laws, the statute in question was within competency of Louisiana Legislature, exercising the police power of the State. The judgment of the Supreme Court of State upholding law was therefore upheld.

Mr. Justice Harlan announced a very vigorous dissent saying that he saw nothing but mischief in all such laws. In his view of the case, no power in the land had right to regulate the enjoyment of civil rights upon the basis of race. It would be just as reasonable and proper, he said, for states to pass laws requiring separate cars to be furnished for Catholic and Protestants, or for descendants of those of Teutonic race and those of Latin race.

So-called Jim Crow Laws replaced slavery with segregation. Here the Supreme Court ruled on the *Plessy v. Ferguson* case that separate railway carriages must be provided for blacks and whites.

Through ruthlessly driving competitors out of business and, at times, sanctioning violence and sabotage, John D. Rockefeller rose to dominance of the oil industry in the 1870s.

was controlled by a political syndicate known as the "Tweed Ring." Two years later, it was discovered that the Union Pacific Railroad had funded the construction of its western railway line at hugely inflated prices. To keep this quiet, shares had been distributed to US congressmen to avoid investigation.

## HARD TIMES

With a manufacturing boom, America quickly became the factory of the world, and cities developed rapidly. The boom, however, came at a price for laborers. Shifts in Pittsburgh's steel mills could be 12 hours a day, seven days a week. And while the first skyscrapers celebrated new wealth, the poor lived in ever more confined conditions. In New York, it was not uncommon for 200 people to live in a single townhouse. By the 1880s, the slums of New York's East Side were said to be twice as densely populated as those of London.

Despite everything, opportunities for work continued to draw immense numbers of immigrants to the US. But it is no surprise that there were labor disputes throughout the final decades of the century—often involving violent clashes with the Pinkerton Detective Agency, hired by the factory owners. In 1877, the bloodiest year, strikes by railroad workers spread to other industries, leading to protests from New York and Pittsburgh across to Ohio and Illinois, and resulting in at least 100 deaths.

# IN THE RE-ENACTMENT AT GETTYSBURG

Where today enthusiasts re-enact battles from long before they were born, at the 50th anniversary of the Battle of Gettysburg in 1913, the veterans played themselves. By then, the youngest veteran was 61 years old.

In the immediate years after the Civil War, few soldiers from either side had participated in veterans's events, but time is a great healer: the 1913 Gettysburg commemoration drew 50,000 people and lasted for six days.

How, though, would the two sides of combatants feel to be facing their former enemies once again? In recreating the assault of July 3, 1863, that had cost more than 7,000 lives, the aging Confederates helped each other across the fields, before reaching the Yankee line, where the Union veterans were waiting. Finally, the Union soldiers surged forward at their old foe—not in combat, but, as Philip Myers, a young observer, noticed, "reunited in brotherly love and affection."

There was still great ill feeling in the South about the war, but on this day, among these men, it was forgotten.

UNDER BLUE & GRAY, GETTYSBURG

Union and Confederate flags held by veterans of the Battle of Gettysburg, 50,000 of whom returned for the action's 50-year commemoration in 1913.

In Chicago in 1893, workers at the Pullman rail plant went on strike when engineer and industrialist George Pullman made wage cuts, but refused a parallel reduction in rents for his workers in his company town. Hoodlums turned the strike into a riot, and the army was sent in, leading to 34 deaths. Then in 1914, the National Guard used the new weapon of machine guns against miners in Colorado, killing 70 people, including women and children.

An English coal-heaver's home in Poverty Gap on New York's Lower East Side, photographed by Jacob Riis in 1890. In good times, the father earned five dollars a week at the city docks.

In addition to the harsh treatment from employers, the law was rarely of any help for workers; for example, the Supreme Court decided in the 1905 Lochner case that New York had no power to regulate the maximum working hours of employees. This was just one of many cases where government regulation of business activities was found to be an infringement of corporate civil rights. As historian David Reynolds writes: "The cities were America's pride and shame, monuments to capital and capitalism, yet also the graveyard of labor."

## THE INDIAN WARS

Across territory occupied by Native Americans, the story was repeatedly one of treaties being ignored and settlers encroaching on Indian land, leading to much bloodshed. Conflict with Native Americans in Texas, largely the Comanche, lasted for 50 years in the middle of the nineteenth century, only ending with the final Comanche moving to reservations in Oklahoma in 1875. In 1862, starving Santee Sioux rebelled against settlers in Minnesota when they had not received the provisions that they had been promised under a US treaty; they killed 700 settlers before the US Army could respond. Three hundred Indians were sentenced to death for the murders. Lincoln commuted most of the sentences, although 38 were hanged, making it the largest mass execution in US history.

In the subduing of the Navajo between 1864 and 1866, 9,000 Native Americans were forced to march from their reservation in Arizona to the Bosque Redondo Reservation, 300 miles (482 km) away in New Mexico. Hundreds died of exhaustion on the way, and it is said some were executed. When they arrived,

**HUNDREDS OF NAVAJO DIED OF EXHAUSTION ON THE FORCED MARCH TO THEIR RESERVATION.**

Bosque Redondo turned out to be overcrowded and the Navajo were forced to join Apaches, a tribe they were not friendly with. The Navajo were also raided by the Comanche, who, in turn, raided them back.

With poor water supplies and with crops failing, the US Army began to incur huge costs in feeding the Indians; the Navajo began leaving in 1867, before the reservation was officially abandoned the following year. In a rare reversal, the US then permitted the Navajo to return to their traditional lands.

## WHERE THE BUFFALO ROAMED

Both white settlers and Plains Indians—with the warring Sioux acting almost like imperialists over other tribes—hunted buffalo to disastrous effect. In the middle of the century, there may have been 60 million buffalo; by 1883, there were fewer than a thousand. For the white Americans who ate some buffalo and hunted them for sport, the elimination of the animal made a perverse kind of sense, as Secretary of the Interior, Columbus Delano, explained to Congress in 1874: "I regard the destruction of such game as Indians subsist upon as facilitating the policy of the Government, of destroying their hunting habits, coercing them on reservations, and compelling them to begin to adopt the habits of civilization." Ridding the Plains of buffalo was a way of ridding them of Native Americans.

## LITTLE BIG HORN AND WOUNDED KNEE

The names of the massacres involving Native Americans over the centuries have largely been forgotten, but "Custer's Last Stand" at Little Big Horn is well known—because it is one of the few cases where white Americans were the victims. In Montana in June 1876, General George Custer's forces from the Seventh Cavalry, supported by Crow Indian scouts, were hugely outnumbered and outmaneuvered by Northern Cheyenne and Arapaho tribes, including leaders Sitting Bull and Crazy Horse. Of more than 200 men whom Custer directly led into battle, none survived. The grim news of Custer's defeat reached the rest of America on July 4—the centenary of the Declaration of Independence.

Little Big Horn, however, proved to be a Pyrrhic victory for the Native Americans, as it stirred white Americans into settling "the Indian problem."

Over the next three years, the major Indian military forces were crushed, while new treaties confiscated vast pieces of land on a "sell or starve" basis. In 1886, even Apache leader Geronimo in Arizona was forced to surrender.

Although billed as Geronimo's last buffalo kill—at Fort Sill in Oklahoma around 1906—this may also have been his first: his earlier hunting experiences in New Mexico and Arizona were unlikely to have brought him into contact with any.

Collecting the bodies of the 150 Indian men, women, and children who had been shot by US troops in the Wounded Knee massacre in South Dakota in 1890. In the confusion, the troops had also killed 25 US soldiers.

A new religion suddenly emerged from the starving and desperate Lakota Indians of South Dakota—the Ghost Dance, one of the tenets of which was the eradication of white settlers. Fearing an attack, the US cavalry decided to hold some chiefs in custody. But in its effort to take Sitting Bull in December 1890, shots were fired, resulting in his death and those of eight of his supporters and six policemen.

Two hundred members of his band joined other Native Americans heading for safety on a reservation, but on the way they were intercepted by US cavalry at Wounded Knee Creek. When the troops tried to search them, a scuffle developed, a shot rang out, and the cavalry began firing. In the shooting, the cavalry killed 150 Indian men, women, and children, including those who tried to flee, while also accidentally firing on their own troops. Twenty-five soldiers died and 39 were wounded in the fighting.

Such massacres had not been uncommon, but Wounded Knee would be one of the last as the Native Americans, their numbers depleted through disease and war, were now limited to scattered reservations. "When I look back from this high hill of my old age, I can still see the butchered women and children lying heaped

**IN THE SHOOTING, THE CAVALRY KILLED 150 INDIAN MEN, WOMEN, AND CHILDREN.**

and scattered all along the crooked gulch," wrote Wounded Knee survivor Black Elk years later. "And I can see that something else died there in the bloody mud, and was buried in the blizzard. A people's dream died there. It was a beautiful dream."

Throughout the nineteenth century, Native Americans had repeatedly been uprooted and shunted onto less productive, more cramped land. As historian Howard Zinn observed, the United States made 400 treaties with the Indians—and broke every one of them.

## SEARCHING FOR CYNTHIA ANN PARKER

Founding Father Benjamin Franklin wondered in 1753 why it was that a Native American child raised by settlers would, if ever allowed to see its Indian relatives, refuse to return to a settler family. But if a settler child were taken prisoner by Indians and "lived awhile among them" it would, having been returned to its white family, "become disgusted with our manner of life" and "take the first good opportunity of escaping again into the woods."

So it was with Cynthia Ann Parker, one of the kidnapped children whose story inspired the movie *The Searchers*. When she was a child, her extended family moved to Texas, building Fort Parker. There, in 1836, a Comanche-led war raid massacred five men in her family, raping the women and cutting the genitals off her grandfather, John Parker, before scalping him. Two women and three children were kidnapped, including Cynthia, aged about 10, and her two-year-old brother, John Richard. The women were gang raped and treated as slaves, but children were regarded as a way to increase the tribe's size and were accepted as tribal members.

After many months, the captive women were freed when Cynthia's uncle, James W. Parker, tracked down the Comanche party and paid ransoms. After six years, John Richard was freed, though he proved unable to adapt to white society and ran away to rejoin his Comanche family.

Cynthia was not found and stayed with different Comanche for 24 years, marrying a chieftain and having three children, one of whom, Quanah, became the last free Comanche chief. When she was about 34, Cynthia was "rescued" by Texas Rangers, but she spent the remaining decade of her life refusing to adjust to life in white society, once escaping temporarily back to her Comanche family. Heartbroken at being separated from her part-Comanche children, she refused to eat and died in 1871.

## HOW THE WEST WAS SPUN

In 1889, the previously Indian land of the Oklahoma territory was opened up to the last great western land rush. On April 22 alone, 50,000 people surged across two million acres of newly available land, staking their claim on what would become their new farmland. With the settlement of Oklahoma, argued historian Frederick Jackson Turner in 1893, the frontier was closed, and so the first period of American history was at an end.

Just over a century old, the United States was a young country in need of a national mythology. It found it in the West. The pioneer spirit had looked to a future in the West; now life in the West could begin to pass into the realm of myths of a recent past. Where old Europe had heroes in medieval knights and honest outlaws like Robin Hood, America's heroes would be cowboys—which was odd, given

**THE UNITED STATES WAS A YOUNG COUNTRY IN NEED OF A NATIONAL MYTHOLOGY.**

how unheroic the life of a cattle herdsman usually was. But, as historian William W. Savage notes: "Everything that has been done to the cowboy has been done, consciously or unconsciously, to make him usable as a myth."

In fiction, in the romantic paintings of Albert Bierstadt and Frederic Remington, and later in movies and on television, cowboys became honorable, courageous, and chivalric, their actions reaching far beyond looking after their bovine charges.

## SHOTGUN HOSPITALITY

Cowboys did not really exist until after the Civil War; it was only then, with the buffalo population almost extinguished, that the cattle indus-

Cynthia Ann Parker with her daughter Topasannah in 1861, shortly after they were "rescued" from the Comanche. Separated from her other part-Comanche children, Parker refused to adjust back to life in white society.

try took off. Cowboys would drive cattle north to railheads, where the cows would be loaded on to trains to take them to the cities of the Midwest for slaughter. Dodge City in Kansas developed as a railhead and was for 10 years the largest cow town in the world. In popular culture, it has a reputation for its outlaw activity. In reality, for all its cowboys and gamblers, saloons and brothels, as well as merchants, bankers and families, there were very few unnatural deaths.

True Western incidents, such as Wyatt Earp's gunfight at the OK Corral in Tombstone, Arizona, in 1881, became famous because they were so uncommon. Villains, saloons, and stagecoaches, let alone ones being held up, were seldom seen. In fact, the racial conflicts in

Louisiana and the South were more violent than the romanticized West during this period.

Admittedly, the West could be lawless—in places there were no lawmen—so communities established committees of vigilance to deal with desperadoes. Sometimes this did descend into mob rule, but usually it involved responsible citizens working against horse thieves, cattle rustlers, and robbers. The most active vigilance committee was at Fort Griffin in Texas, where, in April 1876, they caught a man stealing a horse. Meting out their own form of justice, they promptly hanged him from a tree, leaving below the swinging body a pick and shovel for anyone who might want to bury him.

The feuds of the West, of Billy the Kid and Wyatt Earp, were, as historian Philip Jenkins notes, essentially factional struggles for economic and political power, just like the conflicts in the cities back east. Just as the courts had favored big business in industrial disputes, so they often failed to convict the powerful in the West—such as the Stock Growers Association in their 1892 "war" against homesteaders in Johnson County, Wyoming. In this way, the myths of the Wild West, in which justice was found for the little man outside the law, proved a corrective to the historical injustices often handed down.

The Dodge City Peace Commission of 1883, with Wyatt Earp seated, second from left. Earp has entered the mythology of the West as a celebrated lawman, but he had several run-ins with the law himself.

## THE END OF THE WEST

By the late 1880s, the open land had largely been fenced off by homesteaders. Cattle driving gave way to wheat fields, and towns ironed out

William F. Cody had been an army scout and buffalo hunter before turning his skills to circus entertainment in staging "Buffalo Bill's Wild West." A supporter of Native Americans, Cody called them "the former foe, present friend, the American."

the wilderness and lawlessness. With the Wild West ending, its survivors could move on, some finding work in the myth industry—Wyatt Earp spent his final years advising on Westerns in 1920s' Hollywood. William F. Cody, who had been an army scout, buffalo hunter and Indian fighter, established "Buffalo Bill's Wild West Show," featuring Annie Oakley, which toured America and Britain, performing Western-style circus stunts and historical scenes.

The Wild West, as much as it ever existed, was over. In 1900, artist Frederic Remington wrote to his wife: "I shall never come to the West again—it is all brick buildings."

## THE IMPERIAL AGE

In 1867, Russia sold Alaska to the United States for $7 million, ending its imperial stake in North America. The US, on the other hand, was about to emerge into its own imperialist era. When, in 1895, the people of Cuba launched a nationalist revolution against the Spanish empire, the Spanish suppressed the Cubans, stripping the countryside to deny the revolutionaries access to food and shelter, and herding the people into the towns and cities. US newspapers, particularly popular ones owned by William Randolph Hearst and the Pulitzer chain, were heavily critical of the Spanish action, stirring up popular opinion against the Spanish Empire.

This wasn't just exotic international news for Americans; there was a commercial interest here, too. Cuba, only 90 miles (145 km) from Florida, was home to American sugar and tobacco plantations, and with the Cuban cities rioting, US Marines were sent to protect American residents and property. When, in February 1898, the USS *Maine* exploded in Havana harbor, the same newspapers, feeding war fever, promptly blamed enemy action. A naval court of inquiry concluded that a

The explosion of the USS *Maine* while in Havana harbor in 1898 helped trigger America's war with Spain. An inquiry ruled that the blast was caused by a mine, though it could well have been a technical fault.

submarine mine was responsible, although it could also have been caused by a technical fault on the ship. Nonetheless, war was declared on the Spanish Empire and Cuba soon fell into American hands.

The following month, the US intervened in nationalist movements against the Spanish in the Philippines, taking control of the islands. By the end of the year, America had formally acquired possession of Hawaii, along with the former Spanish colonies of Puerto Rico, the Pacific island of Guam, and the Philippines.

The brief Spanish–American War had seen relatively few American lives lost. But the fighting in the Philippines was not over yet. The next year, the native people of the Philippines began a revolt against the Americans that would take three more years to suppress. Efforts to crush this were brutal, including water torture, prison deaths and concentration camps. By 1900, 70,000 US troops were stationed in the Philippines; when the conflict was over, 4,000 US troops had died, while Filipino fatalities may have reached as many as 250,000.

## THE PANAMA CANAL

Despite the casualties in the Philippines, the Spanish–American War had introduced America as a player on the world stage. Realizing the importance of being able to move warships quickly from the Pacific to the Atlantic, in 1903, President Theodore Roosevelt negotiated to lease land to build a canal in Panama, a region at that time controlled by Colombia. Negotiations were helped by the presence of a US gunboat, followed by an engineered rebellion to create the puppet state of Panama. After that, within two weeks the US had signed the Canal Treaty, winning the right in perpetuity to build and operate a canal through Panama.

To some Americans, acquiring overseas colonies was an extension of the process by which the US had reached across North America, bringing disorganized or weak areas under the protective American wing. But this new position was not universally popular at home. Ben Tillman, a

## SHOOTING THE PRESIDENT

James A. Garfield did not survive for long in the White House. Inaugurated in March 1881, by September he was out of office. On July 2, while heading for a train at the Baltimore and Potomac Railroad Station in Washington, he was shot by Charles J. Guiteau, a disturbed dropout. Garfield fought for his life for three months before dying; Guiteau, who had remained beside the president after the shooting, was hanged the following year.

Twenty years after Garfield's death, on September 6, 1901, President William McKinley was at a public event in Buffalo, New York, when he was shot by 28-year-old anarchist Leon Czolgosz. McKinley's wounds turned gangrenous and he died before his assassin was sent to the electric chair the following month.

Having been started by France in the 1880s, construction of the Panama Canal was taken over by the United States in 1904. By the time it was completed 10 years later, the 48 mile (77 km) project had claimed the lives of 5,600 workers.

senator from South Carolina, criticized efforts to replace Spanish rule in Cuba with American control, calling the US—in a term subsequently hurled, rightly or wrongly, many times at America—"the policeman" of the area.

Nevertheless, when US forces withdrew from Cuba in 1901, the terms of departure effectively made the island an American protectorate, even allowing America to build bases there. One such base would be Guantánamo Bay.

## AMERICA, AMERICA

In the generation after the Civil War, America had become the largest economy in the world, and, with its involvement in Latin America and in the Philippines, it had launched itself as an imperial power. Now the twentieth century would see it involved in huge conflicts on the global stage.

# CHAPTER 3

# THE NEW AGE

ALTHOUGH DETERMINED NOT TO BECOME INVOLVED IN WORLD WAR I, BY 1918 American troops were fighting in the trenches in Europe. The United States would, however, emerge dominant from the war, with its industries booming, while mobsters thrived during Prohibition. Then, in 1929, the bubble would burst.

In August 1914, war broke out in Europe, with Britain, France, and Russia in conflict with the Central Powers of Germany, Austro-Hungary and the Ottoman Empire. The United States was not involved. As in the Napoleonic Wars in the early nineteenth century, it sought only to maintain its neutrality and continue its existing trading patterns with European powers on both sides of the conflict. Furthermore, if it did go to war, which side would America be on? Its population was a melting pot of different people, including Germans, British, Irish, Italians, Czechs, Serbs, and many others—but chiefly, as President Woodrow Wilson observed, "the nations now at war." Neutrality was the obvious path.

However, as with the war of 1812, it proved impossible to remain neutral, and to trade with countries that were at war, because America's merchant ships became military targets. In 1915, Germany abandoned the recognized policy of "stop and search" of civilian ships and began firing indiscriminately at them. Most famously it torpedoed the British Cunard liner *Lusitania*, sailing from New York to Liverpool, killing 1,198 passengers and crew. While Germany claimed, correctly, that the ship had secretly been carrying arms and ammunition to Britain, the sinking prompted an international outcry. Despite the loss of 128 American lives, Wilson remained determined not to be dragged into the war.

For a time, Germany ceased targeting civilian ships, but in early 1917 it resumed torpedoing vessels bound for Britain and France. This was a gamble: would these attacks exhaust British supplies and force Britain to surrender before America could mobilize against

Dorothea Lange's photograph of a migrant farm worker and two of her seven children in Nipomo, California, in March 1936, has become one of the best-known images of the Great Depression.

Germany? They didn't. In March 1917, the interception of the so-called Zimmermann Telegram from the German foreign ministry to the government of Mexico, suggesting a German–Mexican alliance against the US and the reoccupation of Texas and other states that had been lost to America, fueled war fever. On April 6, 1917, Congress voted to declare war on Germany.

## BRAVERY IN THE TRENCHES

Two million American soldiers served in the trenches in France, but because of the training required for new conscripts and a shortage of ships, it was not until summer 1918 that significant numbers of American troops arrived in Europe. Still, in September 1918, a million Americans were part of the Allied Meuse-Argonne campaign, which broke the German lines. Suddenly in November, the war was over, with Germany and its allies exhausted by the economic blockade and crushed by recent offensives. For the US it had been a fairly brief involvement, but casualties

**A MILLION AMERICANS WERE PART OF THE ALLIED MEUSE-ARGONNE CAMPAIGN.**

had been high—as they were for all belligerents—with 116,000 American deaths, fewer than half of them in battle.

The torpedoing of the liner *Lusitania* by a German U-boat off the coast of Ireland in 1915 caused the deaths of 1,198 passengers and crew, including 128 Americans. Despite the international outcry, President Wilson remained determined, at that time, not to be drawn into World War I.

## THE LEAGUE OF NATIONS

The war left Europe exhausted but America a dominant world player. For President Wilson, this was his opportunity to create a new world order of collective security—his "fourteen points" including open seas, limited arms, a recognition of people living under colonial rule, and a "general association of nations" recognizing each country's political independence and territorial integrity.

# AFRICAN-AMERICAN SOLDIERS

Segregation and racial tension in America did not stop with the country going to war. Violence erupted in August 1917 in Houston, Texas, when black soldiers stationed at Camp Logan retaliated against discrimination and abuse from white residents and the police. Marching on the city, the soldiers killed 16 white civilians and police, while four black soldiers died in the fighting. For the offenses, more than 100 soldiers were court-martialed, 63 received life sentences, and 13 were hanged.

Of those who did serve in Europe, most were given service roles rather than combat ones. There were, however, two black combat divisions, the 92nd and 93rd, made up of approximately 40,000 troops. Unease about white Americans fighting alongside black Americans led to the 93rd being loaned to the French Army. Issued with French helmets and weapons, but keeping their US Army uniforms, the 369th Infantry Regiment of the 93rd never lost a trench, retreated, or had a soldier taken prisoner, and only once failed to take an objective.

Private Henry Johnson of the 369th, a former Albany station porter, became the first American to be awarded France's military decoration, the Croix de Guerre. By the end of the war, 171 members of the 369th had received the Croix de Guerre or other French military decorations.

As Native Americans living on reservations had largely been denied citizenship, they couldn't be drafted for military service, but 6,500 Indian men enlisted and served in every major US Army engagement of the war. In 1919, Congress granted automatic citizenship to all Indian war veterans, and in 1924, citizenship was granted to all Indians who had not yet received it.

African-American soldiers in France in 1918.

After lengthy negotiations in Europe, this initiative became the League of Nations, but, despite the war, or as a consequence of it, American feeling remained opposed to becoming entangled in foreign alliances or wars. Ironically, Wilson failed to get US membership of the League of Nations through Congress. It had been his idea and it existed, but he couldn't persuade his own people to sign up for it.

## LYNCHINGS

The war years proved good for American industry, and black Southerners were now increasingly attracted north by better-paid jobs in manufacturing and a chance to escape the South's "Jim Crow" segregation laws. By 1920, 500,000 black Southerners had headed north as part of the Great Migration. During the war years, the black population of Chicago almost doubled, reaching 110,000, but blacks were still discriminated against. In July 1919, a race riot there left 38 people dead. In East St. Louis two years earlier, black strike-breakers had been blamed for the failure of a labor protest, with 100 black people dying in the ensuing violence.

Meanwhile, in the South, the Ku Klux Klan saw a revival; by the early 1920s, the movement had a membership in excess of four million. Blacks were usually the victims of lynchings and burnings, but Asians, Catholics, Jews, and anyone foreign-born could be targeted. The Klan had become an extreme expression of a conservative Southern Protestant backlash against multicultural America.

In May 1916 in Waco, Texas, Jessie Washington, a black teenager, pleaded guilty to murdering his employer, Lucy Fry, a white English farmer. Having received the death sentence, Washington was being led from the dock in Waco's courthouse when spectators surged forward and dragged him outside. Watched by a crowd in front of city hall, Washington was doused in oil, hung from a tree, and repeatedly lowered into the flames of a bonfire, which burned him alive. Although the case was condemned across the country, no one was ever prosecuted for his killing.

THE NEW YORK TIMES, THURSDAY, NOVEMBER 23, 1922.

ADVERTISEMENT          ADVERTISEMENT          ADVERTISEMENT          ADVERTISEMENT

# THE SHAME OF AMERICA

## Do you know that the United States is the Only Land on Earth where human beings are BURNED AT THE STAKE?

### In Four Years, 1918-1921, Twenty-Eight People Were Publicly BURNED BY AMERICAN MOBS

# 3436 People Lynched 1889 to 1922

For What Crimes Have Mobs Nullified Government and Inflicted the Death Penalty?

| The Alleged Crimes | The Victims | Why Some Mob Victims Died: |
|---|---|---|
| Murder | 1288 | Not turning out of road for white boy in auto |
| Rape | 571 | Being a relative of a person who was lynched |
| Crimes against the Person | 615 | Jumping a labor contract |
| Crimes against Property | 333 | Being a member of the Non-Partisan League |
| Miscellaneous Crimes | 453 | "Talking back" to a white man |
| Absence of Crime | 176 | "Insulting" white man. |
| | 3436 | |

## Is Rape the "Cause" of Lynching?

Of 3,436 people murdered by mobs in our country, only 571, or less than 17 per cent., were even *accused* of the crime of rape.

### 83 WOMEN HAVE BEEN LYNCHED IN THE UNITED STATES

Do lynchers maintain that they were lynched for "the usual crime"?

### AND THE LYNCHERS GO UNPUNISHED

# THE REMEDY

## The Dyer Anti-Lynching Bill Is Now Before the United States Senate

The Dyer Anti-Lynching Bill was passed on January 26, 1922, by a vote of 230 to 119 in the House of Representatives

The Dyer Anti-Lynching Bill Provides:
That culpable State officers and mobbists shall be tried in Federal Courts on failure of State courts to act, and that a county in which a lynching occurs shall be fined $10,000, recoverable in a Federal Court.

The Principal Question Raised Against the Bill is upon the Ground of Constitutionality.

The *Constitutionality* of the Dyer Bill Has Been Affirmed by
The Judiciary Committee of the House of Representatives
The Judiciary Committee of the Senate
The United States Attorney General, legal adviser of Congress
Judge Guy D. Goff, of the Department of Justice

The Senate has been petitioned to pass the Dyer Bill by
29 Lawyers and Jurists, including two former Attorneys General of the United States
19 State Supreme Court Justices
24 State Governors
3 Archbishops, 85 bishops and prominent churchmen
39 Mayors of large cities, north and south.

The American Bar Association at its meeting in San Francisco, August 9, 1922, adopted a resolution asking for further legislation by Congress to punish and prevent lynching and mob violence.

Fifteen State Conventions of 1922 (3 of them Democratic) have inserted in their party platforms a demand for national action to stamp out lynchings.

The Dyer Anti-Lynching Bill is not intended to protect the guilty, but to assure to every person accused of crime trial by due process of law.

### THE DYER ANTI-LYNCHING BILL IS NOW BEFORE THE SENATE
### TELEGRAPH YOUR SENATORS TODAY YOU WANT IT ENACTED

If you want to help the organization which has brought to light the facts about lynching, the organization which is fighting for 100 per cent. Americanism, not for some of the people some of the time, but for all of the people, white or black, all of the time

Send your check to J. E. Spingarn, Treasurer of the

# NATIONAL ASSOCIATION FOR THE ADVANCEMENT OF COLORED PEOPLE
70 FIFTH AVENUE, NEW YORK CITY

THIS ADVERTISEMENT IS PAID FOR IN PART BY THE ANTI-LYNCHING CRUSADERS.

An advertisement by the National Association for the Advancement of Colored People (NAACP) urging the US Senate to pass the 1922 Dyer Anti-Lynching Bill. The bill didn't make it through the Senate, being repeatedly blocked by Southern Democrats.

Nor were lynchings limited to the South. In 1930 in Marion, Indiana, Thomas Shipp and Abram Smith were lynched—the photograph of their dangling bodies inspiring the song "Strange Fruit." As far north as Duluth, Minnesota, in 1920, three black circus workers were lynched by a mob after a white 19-year-old girl, Irene Tusken, had accused them of raping and robbing

## JESSIE WASHINGTON WAS DOUSED IN OIL, HUNG FROM A TREE, AND LOWERED INTO THE FLAME OF A BONFIRE.

her. Her doctor could find no evidence of sexual assault, but the same day a mob broke into the jail where the arrested men—Elias Clayton, Elmer Jackson, and Isaac McGhie—were being held. After a sham trial, the men were beaten and hanged. Trial proceedings of the mob opened two days later. Of 25 indictments for rioting, three received convictions and two were tried for rape, with one found guilty. But as with other lynchings, no one was ever convicted for the murders of the lynched men.

Thomas Shipp and Abram Smith were arrested in Marion, Indiana, in 1930, for murdering a white man and raping his white girlfriend. The following evening, they were dragged out of the jail by a mob and lynched.

## ANTI-IMMIGRATION AND 100 PERCENT AMERICANISM

Looking inwardly, the war had generated waves of both patriotism in America and anti-German feeling. Then, with the Bolsheviks taking power in Russia in 1917, there was a small Red Scare in the US (1919–20), when workers, often immigrants, went on strike and vigilante groups emerged to rough them up.

A small anarchist movement also had a violent impact. One parcel bomb sent to a former US senator in May 1919 blew the hands off the maid who opened it. The following month, bombs were let off outside the homes of politicians, with the front of the house of attorney general Mitchell Palmer being blown in. No one inside was seriously hurt, but the bomber, Italian anarchist Carlo Valdinoci, lost his life in the explosion.

Tightening up security, Palmer created a new Bureau of Investigation—a forerunner of the FBI. Raids were made on alien radicals—with 4,000 seized across the country in one night in 1920—and

The home of Attorney General Mitchell Palmer after anarchist Carlo Valdinoci set off a bomb, killing himself in the blast.

people were held without charge. Although these actions were criticized as a breach of civil liberties, 800 were still deported.

Anti-immigrant feeling, even in a nation of immigrants, led to the closure of the open-door policy in the early 1920s—with some exceptions. Latin Americans were still allowed, as migrant Mexican farm labor was needed, and immigration from China and Japan was not completely banned. European immigration, however, fell drastically.

## A DRINK TO PROHIBITION

For decades, evangelical Protestants had campaigned against the sale of alcohol, while Catholics of Irish and German descent had opposed it. But with the anti-German mood during and after the war, the Prohibitionist case was strengthened. Consequently, in January 1920, the Eighteenth Amendment came into force, banning the manufacture, import, and sale of "intoxicating liquors."

Not that Prohibition stopped all America drinking—it just drove it underground, where organized criminals moved in to manage it. For them, Prohibition was a golden opportunity, the profits enabling bootleggers to extend their influence. Unsurprisingly, turf wars broke out, with mass shootings, such as that in Philadelphia in 1928 and on St Valentine's Day in Chicago in 1929, where seven members of the North Side Irish gang were shot dead by four of Al Capone's South Side Italian-American gang. The perpetrators escaped easily: with two

**NOT THAT PROHIBITION STOPPED ALL AMERICA DRINKING—IT JUST DROVE IT UNDERGROUND.**

dressed as policemen, they "escorted" the other two—with their hands up—from the garage, and disappeared into the city before the real police arrived.

In all, Capone may have been responsible for ordering 300 deaths, but it was for tax evasion that he was eventually convicted in 1931. Already suffering from neurosyphilis, he gradually lost his mind while in prison. He died at his Florida home in 1947.

Chicago had been Capone's domain, but in New York by the end of the 1920s, two other factions of Italian-American gangsters had emerged for dominance, one led by Joe Masseria and the other by Salvatore Maranzano. In 1931, Masseria was murdered, leaving Maranzano dominant. To limit disputes, he divided the city's underworld into five families, each with its own turf. But in setting himself up as boss of all bosses, Maranzano seems to have gone a step too far. Within six months he was murdered on the orders of Charles "Lucky" Luciano—who was supposedly one of his followers.

Luciano brought in a new era of collaboration with other criminal groups, such as Jewish mobsters Meyer Lansky and Ben "Bugsy" Siegel.

The St Valentine's Day Massacre, Chicago, 1929. In a turf war, Al Capone's South Side Italian-American bootleggers shot dead seven members of Bugsy Moran's North Side Irish gang.

Elsewhere, racketeer and political boss Enoch L. "Nucky" Johnson rose to power in Atlantic City, New Jersey, where the liquor laws went largely unenforced.

When Prohibition ended in 1933, the mobsters sought new ventures. Some worked their way into unions and labor rackets, while others moved into narcotics, gambling, and prostitution. They didn't go away; they just diversified.

## FIRE AND WATER IN CALIFORNIA

Far more destructive than the earthquake in San Francisco in 1906 were the fires that followed it. Caused by ruptured gas mains, the fires burned for four days and nights, destroying, along with the earthquake, 80 percent of the city's mainly wooden buildings and killing 3,000 people. In a few cases, residents were motivated not to put the fires out, some even starting them—as insurers didn't indemnify against earthquakes, but did against fire damage. San Francisco

**CAUSED BY RUPTURED GAS MAINS, THE SAN FRANCISCO FIRES BURNED FOR FOUR DAYS.**

was quickly rebuilt, but in the following decades it lost its standing as the West Coast's largest city to Los Angeles.

With oil and, from 1914, a rapidly expanding movie industry, L.A. was growing quickly, but it lacked one vital natural resource: fresh water. Dry in summer and not much wetter in winter, Los Angeles receives less rainfall than some deserts. So where does the city get its water?

The answer, of course, is that it pipes it in. The man largely responsible was William Mulholland, the Belfast-born, self-taught chief engineer of Los Angeles's Bureau of Water Works and Supply. His name is memorialized in Mulholland Drive, the city's winding, tree-lined road and the home to some of Hollywood's biggest stars. But in bringing the water to L.A., and therefore enabling the city to grow and its gardens to look so wonderfully verdant, a great price was paid elsewhere in California.

That was in the Owens Valley, 230 miles (370 km) north of L.A., where the snowmelt from the Sierra Nevada provided plenty of surplus water for local farmlands. Quietly, in the first decade of the twentieth century, Mulholland's men began buying up farmland—and the water rights that went with each plot—not letting on that this was on behalf of the City of Los Angeles. With the land acquired, Mulholland then began building an aqueduct to link the Owens Valley with Los Angeles.

Completed in 1913, the Los Angeles Aqueduct remains a feat of civil engineering, using gravity to carry water down through the Mojave

The 1906 San Francisco Earthquake, and the fires that followed, left at least 227,000 people—more than half the city's population—without homes. The earthquake also permanently diverted the lower course of the Salinas River by 6 miles (9.6 km).

Desert to L.A. But the more the city grew, the more water it demanded. Farmers in the Owens Valley realized that it was taking the water they needed for their farms and that the Owens Lake—originally 12 miles (19 km) long and 8 miles (13 km) wide—was emptying. In protest, the aqueduct was dynamited a number of times. Nevertheless, by 1926 the Owens Lake was dry. Today, noxious soda ash and carcinogenic nickel blow off the lakebed. It is America's largest single source of dust pollution, and a large cleanup operation has been running since the 1990s.

Part of the system that brought water across the desert to supply the city of Los Angeles, the St. Francis Dam collapsed in 1928, flooding the valley beneath it and causing the deaths of 425 people.

Despite the ill feeling in the Owens Valley, in the 1920s Mulholland was still fêted in L.A.—until his reputation was shaken by a disaster closer to home. In the San Francisquito Canyon, 40 miles (64 km) north of Los Angeles, Mulholland and his team built the St. Francis Dam. Copying their design from a textbook, but not modifying it when they increased the dam's capacity without strengthening its walls, their structure was unsound. Opened in 1926, the dam collapsed one night two years later, flooding the valley beneath it and killing 425 people. The disaster remains California's second greatest loss of life after the San Francisco earthquake. Although no one was found to be individually responsible, Mulholland blamed himself, retiring the following year and withdrawing from public life.

**THE DAM COLLAPSED, FLOODING THE VALLEY BENEATH IT AND KILLING 425 PEOPLE.**

Today, with a population of more than four million, a third of Los Angeles's water is still provided by Mulholland's aqueduct—but the city's environmental position remains precarious, with droughts and forest fires persistent concerns.

## HOLLYWOOD

Having opened its first studio in 1914, Hollywood was the heart of American film-making by the end of the decade. While other cities were mass-producing cars or consumer goods, Los Angeles' mass production was movies. The first stars, such as Mary Pickford and Charlie Chaplin, emerged—and, soon learning the value of their popular appeal, they negotiated lucrative contracts for themselves.

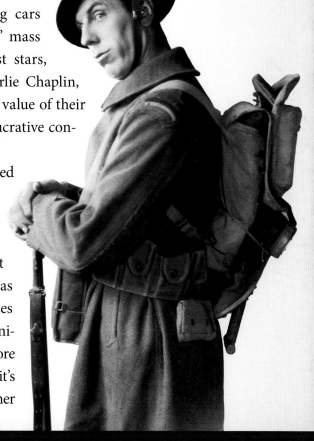

But, being highly paid, loved by the masses, fawned over by employers and, at heart, acutely aware of the fickle nature of fame, makes stardom a volatile mix. It should be little surprise that just as Hollywood magnifies its stars' faces across the big screen, it also magnifies their lives, making them more vulnerable to excesses, whether it's alcohol, drugs, sex, or any other

Karl Dane was a silent comedy Hollywood star, but, with the coming of sound movies in 1928, his Danish accent proved unpopular and his career collapsed. With subsequent ventures failing, he shot himself in 1934.

self-destructive indulgence. When a star's moment has passed, the downfall can be brutal. With the coming of sound films in 1928, silent comedy star Karl Dane's career faltered. With his strong Danish accent unpopular with audiences, he was dropped by MGM and by 1934 was selling hot dogs outside Paramount Pictures. He shot himself soon after.

Many went west to Tinseltown seeking fame and fortune, only to be disappointed. Successful stage actress Peg Entwistle did manage to become known in Hollywood, but not for her movies. Not having been signed by a studio in 1932, she climbed to the top of the Hollywood sign and threw herself off.

## TINSELTOWN'S GREATEST SCANDAL

We don't know his movies anymore, but Roscoe "Fatty" Arbuckle is notorious for his involvement in one of Hollywood's most famous scandals. An immensely popular silent movie comedian earning $1 million a year, Arbuckle is remembered for the story that he killed an actress in a sordid sex act. Except that he didn't.

When Virginia Rappe fell ill at a party that Arbuckle was holding in San Francisco in 1921, she was seen by a doctor, who diagnosed no complaint other than her being drunk. Two days later, Rappe died of peritonitis caused by a ruptured bladder. Bambina Maude Delmont, who had attended the party with Rappe, went on the offensive, claiming that Arbuckle had raped Rappe, who allegedly had said that Arbuckle had hurt her. Was Delmont hoping to extort the movie star? Well, she did have previous convictions for extortion.

Rappe's manager embellished the tale, stating that Arbuckle had used a piece of ice to simulate sex with Rappe. By the time this was reported in the Press, the ice had become a bottle that broke, inflicting fatal internal wounds. Even before the final verdict, Delmont was profiting from the case, touring the country with a show about the scandal. With so much misinformation being circulated, could Arbuckle receive a fair trial?

Not until it was too late. Although the rape and murder charges were quickly dropped, a manslaughter charge remained. Arbuckle went through three trials; the first two juries reached deadlock, with mistrials declared. The third trial found him not guilty, its jury even writing a letter of apology to the star, finding him "entirely innocent."

Movie star Roscoe "Fatty" Arbuckle was supported by his wife Minta Durfee during his trial for manslaughter in 1921. In all, Arbuckle went through three trials before being found not guilty, but the scandal had already ruined his career.

Innocent, yes, but Hollywood had already washed its hands of the sullied star. Arbuckle did later return to occasional work, but, a broken man and now an alcoholic, he died of a heart attack in 1933.

After stories like Arbuckle's, Hollywood made an effort to clean up its act—not by behaving better, but by hushing things up. Whereas today public access to stars' lives is closely con-

**DELMONT WAS ALREADY PROFITING FROM THE ARBUCKLE CASE, TOURING THE COUNTRY WITH A SHOW ABOUT THE SCANDAL.**

trolled by publicists, from the 1920s to the 1950s it was the studios who guarded the stars on their books. Studio fixers, such as MGM's Eddie Mannix, kept scandals out of the public eye by maintaining close relations with Los Angeles's District Attorney Buron Fitts—MGM's head Louis B. Mayer was the top donor to Fitts's re-election campaign—and in buying silence by putting bartenders, hospital staff and policemen on the studio payroll. It is also believed that the fixers may have even covered up murders, with the alleged suicides of Jean Harlow's husband, Paul Bern, in 1932, and George Reeves, star of TV's *The Adventures of Superman*, in 1959, never being wholly convincing.

## THE WALL STREET CRASH

After World War I, the US may have become politically inward-looking, but financially it was open to the world. It invested heavily in Europe, while in trade America became the world's leading exporter and, after Britain, the second largest importer. The automobile and its related industries in petrol and rubber for tires, in particular, were booming.

By the mid-1920s, the economy was growing at around 7 percent a year, while share values on the New York Stock Exchange increased 15-fold between 1923 and 1929. There were warnings that the market was overheating, but, with things going so well, they were ignored. Then in October 1929 the bubble burst. A week of panic-selling cut a

A crowd outside the New York Stock Exchange on October 24, 1929, as selling intensified in the days preceding the Wall Street crash. In the Depression that followed, unemployment would reach almost 24 percent.

## THE BONUS MARCHERS

During the summer of 1932, 20,000 unemployed war veterans moved on Washington, setting up temporary shacks in the city and demanding that the government pay them now a bonus that had been promised for 1945. It was largely peaceful until some agitators whipped things up. The army sent in tanks and tear gas, setting fire to the shacks and leaving two veterans shot dead and two infants asphyxiated by the gas. There was widespread outrage at the heavy-handed response, but Army Chief of Staff, Douglas MacArthur, argued that his actions had stopped more damaging situations developing.

The Bonus Marchers camped out on the US Capitol lawn in Washington, DC, in June 1932.

third off the value of the market. This in itself didn't sink America into depression, because only one percent of the population owned shares, but it was an indicator of the changing economic climate. People began tightening their belts.

With spending on consumer goods falling by 20 percent in 1930 alone, factories closed and workers were laid off, leading to people defaulting on mortgage payments and loans. This exposed another weakness in the US:

with no central bank, local banks were allowed only limited reserves and were highly vulnerable. When the crash caused a run on the banks, they had no one to turn to and closed—with millions of Americans seeing their savings disappear. Between 1929 and 1933—Herbert Hoover's presidency—20 percent of America's banks closed. In some places, people resorted to a barter economy.

Nor did it stop there. With America cutting back on lending overseas and raising tariffs on foreign imports, the Depression deepened around the world. In the US, shantytowns for the homeless—nicknamed "Hoovervilles" after President Hoover—grew up around major cities.

In 1933–35, Depression conditions worsened when drought and high winds hit the farms of the Midwest. With newly mechanized farming methods having already caused soil erosion, parts of the Great Plains were turned into a dust bowl. Some people died from dust pneumonia, others starved and, by 1940, 2.5 million people had left the Plains states. Thousands of ruined farmers trekked west from Arkansas and Oklahoma to seek work in California.

## THE NEW DEAL

When Franklin D. Roosevelt was inaugurated as president in March 1933, a quarter of the US workforce was unemployed and banks had closed in 38 states. Quickly, Roosevelt repealed Prohibition and managed to get many of the banks reopened, reassuring the country that their money was better in banks than under the mattress. Already, the mood was looking a little more buoyant. That summer, the Glass-Steagall Act separated investment banks from those handling loans and deposits, the blurring of the two having contributed to the Crash and the Depression—as it would in the financial crisis of 2008. In taking America off the gold standard, Roosevelt devalued the dollar, generating a demand for now cheaper US exports.

# THE MOB IN THE DREAM FACTORY

Hollywood could be corrupting, but it could also be corrupted. After the ending of Prohibition, some mobsters moved west, looking for a new racket. First they infiltrated the projectionists' union, causing strikes, and later they moved in on the movie technicians' union, the 12,000-strong IATSE (International Alliance of Theatrical Stage Employees). With Chicago mobster muscle having ensured they were voted in to run the union, George Browne and Willie Bioff established themselves in their new roles by leaning on the Hollywood studios for backhanders. With the major Hollywood studios each paying the duo $50,000 a year and smaller studios each paying $25,000, Browne and Bioff only pushed for minimal advances in their workers' rights. Meanwhile, union members would have to contribute two percent of wages to a union fund: two-thirds of this went to the Chicago mob, and the rest to Bioff and Browne's own pockets.

**HOLLYWOOD COULD BE CORRUPTING, BUT IT COULD ALSO BE CORRUPTED.**

The wreckage after mobster Willie Bioff was killed by a car bomb in Phoenix, Arizona, in 1955.

What brought Bioff and Browne down was their effort to expand and take over the Screen Actors' Guild (SAG). When Robert Montgomery, the guild's president, hired private detectives to investigate Bioff, it quickly came to light that Bioff had not served a sentence for procuring a prostitute in Chicago in 1922, and that Joe Schenck, Chairman of 20th Century Fox, had paid him $100,000. What, the public might wonder, was the chairman of a movie studio doing paying a union leader $100,000?

After more investigations, Schenck and Bioff were brought to trial in 1941. Agreeing to give evidence against Bioff, Schenck served only four months for bribery, before being released back to Fox. There, aged 69, he began a relationship with teenage starlet Marilyn Monroe.

To escape a long sentence in Alcatraz for tax evasion and racketeering, Bioff, in turn, agreed to testify against the Chicago Mafia. This led to indictments against a number of mobsters, including Frank "the Enforcer" Nitti, who shot himself the day his indictment was handed down. Others received 10-year sentences, while Bioff and Browne were paroled after three. Bioff went to live quietly in Phoenix, Arizona, where, one day in 1955, someone left a bomb under his car. The murder has never been solved.

To counteract the effects of the Dust Bowl, laws were put in place to conserve soil and to plant more than 200 million trees from Canada to Texas. The federal government began a massive program of work relief, employing people in construction projects, in teaching and in public libraries. In 1935, unemployment pay was introduced—with, across the

President Franklin D. Roosevelt (*left*), with Secretary of Agriculture Henry A. Wallace, during a White House radio broadcast about the New Deal Farm Programs in July 1940.

decade, more than a third of the population receiving public aid of some kind. America was getting back on its feet.

## THE WINDS OF WAR

Internationally, the mid-1930s saw America at its most isolationist. Where Woodrow Wilson had hoped and failed to make the US a major player in maintaining world peace, the 1935–37 Neutrality Acts worked to keep America out of any foreign entanglements, making it illegal to sell arms or make loans to belligerent nations.

Once again American neutrality was declared when war broke out in Europe in September 1939. But the United States had said that in 1914, too. Then, on December 7, 1941, the Japanese attacked the US naval base at Pearl Harbor in Hawaii, and America went to war once more.

# GLOSSARY

**anarchist** A person who believes in anarchism or anarchy, and who rebels against any authority, established government, or governing power.

**Bonus Marchers** Referring to the 20,000 unemployed war veterans who marched on Washington in 1932 and set up temporary shacks in the city where they squatted, demanding that the government pay them a previously promised bonus now instead of in 1945 as previously stated.

**Compromise of 1850** A series of actions passed by the US Congress, which attempted to balance the number of free states and slave states entering the Union.

**Confederacy** The 11 southern states that seceded from the United States in 1860 and 1861 and would fight the Union in the American Civil War.

**frontier** The extreme margins of settled land or civilization beyond which is either unsettled or unexplored, though, the term particularly refers to much of the western US before Pacific settlement.

**Hoovervilles** Nicknamed for US president Herbert Hoover during the Great Depression, these were communities where people in poverty lived, also known as shanty towns.

**Jim Crow laws** Laws that segregated black and white people in public places.

**scandal** Referring to a loss or damage to reputation caused by public awareness of indiscretions or to the situations of indiscretion in which there are usually moral or legal failings.

**Union** A term for the federal union of states during the period of the American Civil War that did not secede and fought the Confederacy.

**vigilante** Any self-appointed person or people who undertake law enforcement in their community without legal authority by acting on their own, often viewing existing legal authorities as inefficient, corrupt, or inadequate.

# FOR MORE INFORMATION

**Association for the Study of African American Life and History**
Howard Center
2225 Georgia Ave. NW, Ste. 331
Washington, DC 20059
(202) 238-5910
Website: https://asalh100.org
The ASALH, established in 1915 and responsible for founding Black History Month, promotes research and communication of all kinds on Black History and culture in society.

**Canadian Historical Association**
1912-130 Albert Street
Ottawa, ON, K1P 5G4
(613) 233-7885
Website: https://www.cha-shc.ca
The largest historical association in Canada, the CHA encourages research, teaching, charitable events, and connecting historians around the world for the sake of educating all interested persons on the history of Canada.

### The Canadian Museum of History

00 Laurier Street
Gatineau, QC K1A 0M8, Canada
(819) 776-7000
Website: http://www.historymuseum.ca
The exhibits and artifacts for adults and children alike tell of Canada's personal and world histories, including its history in relation to the United States in eras such as the Great Depression

### Economic History Association

Department of Economics, University of Arizona
PO Box 210108
Tucson, AZ 85721-0108
(520) 621-4421
Website: http://eh.net/eha
The EHA promotes teaching, research, and publication on the history of economics in each significant era as it relates to modern-day practice and education.

### The National Civil War Museum

One Lincoln Circle at Reservoir Park
Harrisburg, PA 17103
(717) 260-1861
Website: http://www.nationalcivilwarmuseum.org
This museum chronicles the complete time line of the Civil War and includes detailed prewar period among exhibits on slavery, the authentic experiences of soldiers, and western expansion.

### Smithsonian National Museum of the American Indian

Alexander Hamilton U.S. Custom House
One Bowling Green
New York, NY 10004
(212) 514-3700
Website: http://www.nmai.si.edu

This museum collects Native American history and artifacts to tell the story of migration, settlement, culture, and all major events throughout Native American history.

**Society of Civil War Historians**
George and Ann Richards Civil War Era Center
Penn State Univ., 108 Weaver Bldg.
University Park, PA 16802-5500
(919) 962-4201
Website: http://scwhistorians.org/Scholars who are a part of this society explore and research Civil War, slavery, and other matters of the general era from the 1830s to 1880, with annual meetings in June and quarterly publications.

# FURTHER READING

Davies, Philliop John, and Iwan Morgan. *Hollywood and the Great Depression: American Film, Politics, and Society in the 1930s.* Edinburgh University Press, 2016.

Domingues da Silva, Daniel B. *The Atlantic Slave Trade from West Central Africa, 1780–1867.* (Cambridge Studies on the African Diaspora.) New York, NY: Cambridge University Press, 2017.

Greene, Allison Collis. *No Depression in Heaven: The Great Depression, the New Deal, and the Transformation of Religion in the Delta.* New York, NY: Oxford University Press, 2016.

Gumpert, Mariah, and James Olson. *The Great Depression and the New Deal: Key Themes and Documents.* Santa Barbara, CA: ABC-CLIO—ABC-CLIO, LLC., 2017.

Hahn, Steven. *A Nation Without Borders: The United States and Its World in an Age of Civil Wars, 1830–1910.* (The Penguin History of the United States.) New York, NY: Viking—Penguin Random House LLC., 2016.

Harper, Gordon. *The Fights on the Little Horn: Unveiling the Mysteries of Custer's Last Stand.* Havertown, PA: Casemate Publishers, 2014.

Jeansonne, Glen. *Herbert Hoover: A Life.* New York, NY: Berkley—Penguin Random House, LLC., 2016.

Parker, Nate. *The Birth of a Nation: Nat Turner and the Making of a Movement.* New York, NY: Altria Books—Simon and Schuster, Inc., 2016.

Reséndez, Andrés. *The Other Slavery: The Uncovered Story of Indian Enslavement in America*. New York, NY: Houghton Mifflin Harcourt Publishing Company, 2016.

Salafia, Matthew. *Slavery's Borderland: Freedom and Bondage Along the Ohio River*. (Early American Studies.) Philadelphia, PA: University of Pennsylvania Press, 2013.

# INDEX

**A**

abolition, 10, 12, 15, 18, 32
Allied army, 58
Antietam, Battle of, 20
anti-immigration, 63–64
Apache, 43, 45
Appomattox, 30–31
Arbuckle, Roscoe, 70–72

**B**

black soldiers, 22, 59
Bonus Marchers, 74
Booth, John Wilkes, 31
Brown, John, 15
buffalo, 44, 49
Bull Run, Battle of, 17–18

**C**

Capone, Al, 64–65
Carnegie, Andrew, 26, 38
carpetbaggers, 36
Civil Rights Act of 1875, 34, 38
Civil War, 7–32, 33, 41, 49
Comanche, 43, 47–48

Compromise of 1850, 18
Confederacy, 16–30, 34, 41
Craft, Ellen, 8–9
Craft, William, 8–9
Crazy Horse, 44
Cuba, 52–53, 55
Custer, George, 44

**D**

Davis, Jefferson, 20
Douglas, Stephen, 12
Douglass, Frederick, 22, 29, 34
Dust Bowl, 77

**E**

Earp, Wyatt, 49–51
Emancipation Proclamation, 20–22
Everett, Edward, 24

**F**

Fillmore, Millard, 9
Forest, Bedford, 26
Fort Pillow, Battle of, 26
Fourteenth Amendment, 34, 38

## G

Garfield, James, 54
Geronimo, 45
Gettysburg, 27, 28
Gettysburg, Battle of, 22–23, 41
Gettysburg Address, 24
Glass-Steagall Act, 75
Grant, Ulysses S., 18, 28
Great Depression, 7, 74–75
Great Migration, 60

## H

Harper's Ferry, 15
Hearst, William Randolph, 52
Hollywood, 7, 69–72, 76
Hoover, Herbert, 75
Hoovervilles, 75
hot-air balloons, 25

## I

Imperial Age, 52–53

## J

Jim Crow laws, 38, 60

## K

Kansas-Nebraska Act, 12
Ku Klux Klan, 26, 36–38, 60

## L

Lakota, 46
League of Nations, 58, 60

Lee, Robert E., 18–20, 22–23, 28, 30
Lincoln, Abraham, 12, 15–16,
  19–20, 24, 26, 28–32, 43
Little Big Horn, 44–45
Los Angeles Aqueduct, 67–69
lynchings, 60, 62

## M

*Maine*, 52
McKinley, William, 54
Meade, George, 22
Missouri Compromise, 12
mobsters, 64–66 , 76
Morgan, J.P., 26
Mulholland, William, 66–69

## N

Native Americans, 7, 12, 31, 43–47,
  51, 53, 59
Navajo, 43–44
Neutrality Acts, 78
New York riots, 26–27

## O

OK Corral, 49
Oklahoma territory, 48–49

## P

Palmer, Mitchell, 63
Panama Canal, 53, 55
Parker, Cynthia Ann, 47–48
Pearl Harbor, 78
Pinkerton Detective Agency, 40

plantations, 11, 20, 34, 52
Plessy, Homer, 38–39
Prohibition, 7, 56, 64–66, 76
Pullman rail plant, 42

## R

Rappe, Virginia, 70
Reconstruction, 37
Red Scare, 63
Rockefeller, John D., 26, 38
Roosevelt, Franklin D., 75
Roosevelt, Theodore, 53

## S

San Francisco earthquake of 1906,
  66
Santee Sioux, 43
Scott, Dred, 12–13, 34
sharecropping, 38–39
Shiloh, Battle of, 18–19
Sitting Bull, 44, 46
slavery, 7–16, 18–20, 22, 24, 26,
  28–29, 31–33, 34, 37–39, 48
Spanish–American War, 53
stock market crash of 1929, 7, 72,
  74, 75
submarines, 25
Sumter, Fort, 16

## T

Thirteenth Amendment, 29, 32, 34

## U

Union, 16–29, 32, 41
Union Pacific Railroad, 40

## V

Vanderbilt, Cornelius, 39

## W

Wild West, 7, 49–51
Wilson, Woodrow, 60, 78
World War I, 7, 25, 56–60
Wounded Knee, 46–47

## Z

Zimmerman telegram, 57